W9-CIP-507

BASKETBALL
THE MATH OF THE GAME

BY THOMAS K. ADAMSON

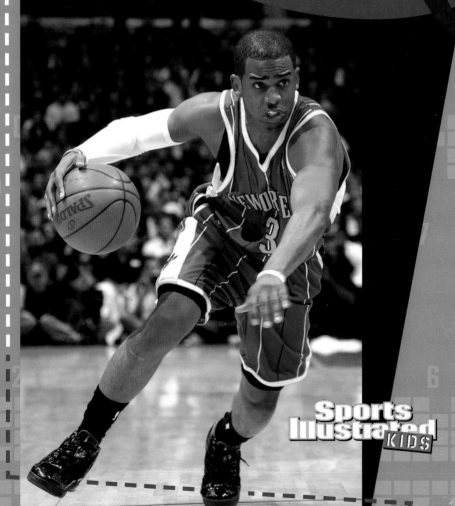

CAPSTONE PRESS
a capstone imprint

Sports Illustrated KIDS Sports Math is published by Capstone Press,
1710 Roe Crest Drive, North Mankato, Minnesota 56003.
www.capstonepub.com
Copyright © 2012 by Capstone Press, a Capstone imprint. All rights reserved.
No part of this publication may be reproduced in whole or in part, or stored in a
retrieval system, or transmitted in any form or by any means, electronic, mechanical,
photocopying, recording, or otherwise, without written permission of the publisher or,
where applicable, Time Inc.
For information regarding permission, write to Capstone Press,
1710 Roe Crest Drive, North Mankato, Minnesota 56003.

SI Kids is a trademark of Time Inc. Used with permission.

Library of Congress Cataloging-in-Publication Data
Adamson, Thomas K., 1970–
  Basketball : the math of the game / by Thomas K. Adamson.
    p. cm.—(Sports illustrated KIDS. Sports math)
  Includes bibliographical references and index.
  Summary: "Presents the mathematical concepts involved with the sport of
basketball"—Provided by publisher.
  ISBN 978-1-4296-6568-1 (library binding)
  ISBN 978-1-4296-7317-4 (paperback)
  ISBN 978-1-4765-0166-6 (e-book)
  1. Basketball—Mathematics—Juvenile literature. I. Title. II. Series.
  GV885.1.A33 2012
  796.35701'51—dc22   2011007863

Editorial Credits
Anthony Wacholtz, editor; Alison Thiele, designer; Eric Gohl, media researcher;
  Eric Manske, production specialist

Photo Credits
Shutterstock/Debra Hughes, design element; Gheorghe Roman, cover
  (back); Petr Vaclavek, design element; Rocket400 Studio, 34 (bottom), 42 (bottom)
Sports Illustrated/Andy Hayt, 15; Bill Frakes, 8, 16, 21 (bottom), 43; Bob
  Rosato, 7 (bottom), 9, 34 (top), 39 (top & bottom left); Damian Strohmeyer, 10–11,
  13 (bottom), 22, 23 (bottom), 28, 36; David E. Klutho, 14 (top), 21 (top), 27, 37, 39
  (bottom right); Hy Peskin, 6; John Biever, 18, 32–33, 38; John G. Zimmerman, 7
  (top); John W. McDonough, cover (front), 1, 4–5, 12–13, 17, 23 (top), 24, 25 (all),
  29, 30, 31, 40, 41, 42 (top), 44, 45; Manny Millan, 14 (bottom); Peter Read Miller,
  35; Robert Beck, 19

Printed in the United States of America in North Mankato, Minnesota.
042015   008920R

TABLE OF CONTENTS

CHAPTER 1

AROUND THE COURT

The exciting, fast-paced sport of basketball is a good place to look for math. Angles and measurements abound, and of course, the players' performances can be measured in statistics. Math can even help you improve your game. Bring some solid numbers to the court and you can become a better player—and a better fan too!

Let's begin by examining the court itself. For the National Basketball Association and college, 10 players have to fit on a rectangular court that measures 94 feet long by 50 feet wide. How much area do the players have to work with?

The area of a rectangle is the base times the height.

$$area = b * h$$

$$area = 50 \text{ feet} * 94 \text{ feet}$$

$$area = 4{,}700 \text{ square feet}$$

94 ft

NBA and college basketball courts have an area of 4,700 square feet. The base and height are measured in feet, but when you multiply them together, the measurement becomes square feet.

Another way to measure a shape is by its perimeter, the distance around the outside of the shape. To find the perimeter of a basketball court, add the lengths of all four sides. Because the court is a rectangle, you can also multiply the base and the height by two. Then add the two numbers together.

$$perimeter = 2b + 2h$$

$$perimeter = 2 * 50 + 2 * 94$$

When you work out a math equation, there's a certain order to follow. You should work on the problem from left to right. More importantly, you need to follow the order of operations. That means that work inside parentheses should be done first. Next are the exponents, such as if a number is squared (x^2). Multiplication and division come next, followed by addition and subtraction.

Because anything inside parentheses is done first, you can add parentheses to help you follow the order of operations. With the perimeter of a basketball court, we can put parentheses around the two multiplication problems because those are done before the addition.

$$P = (2 * 50) + (2 * 94)$$

$$P = 100 + 188$$

$$P = 288 \text{ feet}$$

THE WIDENING LANE

Some court dimensions changed because of the dominance of one player. Before the 1951–1952 NBA season, the lane had a circle with a diameter of 12 feet. The lane itself was only 6 feet wide.

In the late 1940s and early 1950s, George Mikan of the Lakers could set up next to the lane, take a high pass from a teammate, and easily lay the ball in. The NBA widened the lane to make it a bit harder for Mikan to dominate.

Let's calculate the area of the key after the Mikan rule change. First find the area of the circle. The formula for finding the area of a circle is

$$area = \pi * r^2$$

The circle's diameter is 12 feet. To find the area of the circle, we'll use 6 feet in the equation because the radius is half the diameter. Pi is 3.14159 or 3.14.

$$area = 3.14 * 6^2$$
$$area = 3.14 * 36$$
$$area = 113$$

The lane was widened to 12 feet before the 1951–1952 season.

Finding the area of the lane after it was widened is a simple base times height calculation. The lane was 19 feet long and 12 feet wide.

$$area = 19 * 12 \qquad area = 228 \; square \; feet$$

Now we can figure out the area of the entire key, which is the lane plus the free throw half circle. Half the area of the circle is 113 / 2, or 56.5 square feet. Add the rectangle area (228 square feet), and the total area of the key after the rule change was 284.5 square feet.

Was the 228 square feet of paint a large enough area to keep the big men from dominating the game? Not quite. A player named Wilt Chamberlain was able to command the area. The center forced another rule change that increased the area of the key. To open up the inside game, the NBA widened the lane from 12 feet to 16 feet for the 1964–1965 season.

WILT CHAMBERLAIN

How much more area was added to the key? We already know the area of the half circle, 56.5 square feet. We just need the new area of the lane.

*current area of the lane =
16 * 19 = 304 square feet*

*current area of the key =
304 + 56.5 = 360.5 square feet*

12 Ft

16 ft

19 ft

MIAMI HEAT

PUT MORE ARC ON IT!

The goal of basketball is simple: Get the ball through the hoop. Why does that seem so difficult sometimes? Let's get some basic measurements to find out.

Compare the diameter of the rim to the diameter of the basketball. The rim is 18 inches in diameter and the ball is about 9 inches in diameter. So the diameter of the rim is twice as long as the diameter of the ball.

But the ball doesn't cover half as much area as the rim. We have to find the area of each circle. The radius is half the diameter. So to find the area of the rim, we'll use the length of the rim's radius (9 inches) in the equation.

$$area = 3.14 * 9^2$$
$$area = 254.34 \text{ square inches}$$

The area of the rim is about 254 square inches. Use the formula again to find the area of the ball. The radius of the ball is about 4.5 inches.

$$area = 3.14 * 4.5^2$$
$$area = 63.59 \text{ square inches}$$

So the rim has four times as much area as the ball at its widest point. Seems like plenty of space for the ball to go through, right?

If you looked at the rim from the ball's point of view, it would seem as if the rim changes shape as the ball approaches the hoop. If the ball is directly above the rim, the hoop would look like a perfect circle. But the rim looks like a thin oval if the ball is in front of or beside the rim. You want to give the ball the best angle to go through the hoop, which is directly above the basket.

However, you have to get it up over the rim first, and the ball is bouncy. It can bounce and roll all over the rim and fall off without going through the net. That's why basketball players use arc with their shots.

JOSH SMITH

Arc is part of a curve. When a coach tells a player that he needs more arc on his shot, the player needs to send his shot on a higher trajectory. That gives the ball a better angle to go through the hoop.

BANK SHOTS

Ready to learn how to consistently make bank shots? First we have to learn about angles.

The basketball court has a lot of 90-degree angles, which are also called right angles. They look like the corners of a square. A straight line is a 180-degree angle. If you cut that line in half, you get a 90-degree angle. Cut that angle in half and you get a 45-degree angle.

90°

When the ball bounces off a surface, such as the backboard or the floor, the angle it hits will be the same angle it comes off the surface (as long as there is no spin on the ball). So when you bounce the ball straight down at the floor it will bounce straight back up. If it bounces at a 45-degree angle, it will leave at a 45-degree angle. This is where the bank shot comes in.

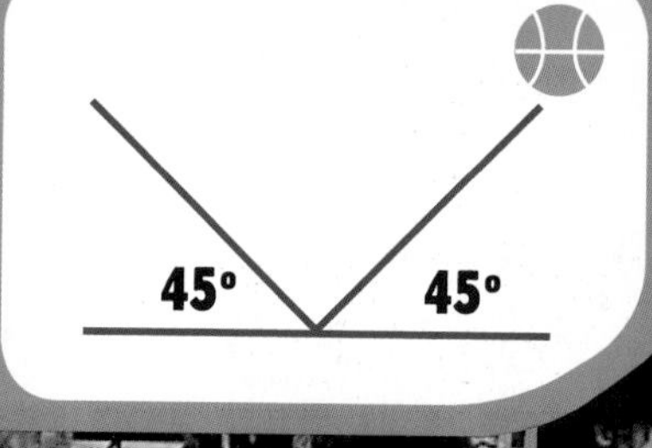

45°   45°

When you're at a 45-degree angle to the backboard, it's a perfect time for a bank shot. If the ball hits the backboard at a 45-degree angle, it will leave the backboard at the same angle. Most of the time, if you aim for the square on the backboard from a 45-degree angle, your shot will go right in the hoop.

You can make bank shots from other angles as well, but it's a little more tricky. For example, a 90-degree angle of the ball to the backboard will send the ball right back at you. Usually if a player makes a bank shot from a 90-degree angle, it's by accident.

You can hit a bank shot from anywhere except the sides of the court. From the sides, you are at a 180-degree angle to the backboard, so you don't have room to bank it in.

A circle has 360 degrees, so it has four 90-degree angles.

90° 90°

90° 90°

3-POINTER DISTANCES

A 3-pointer can electrify the crowd and deflate the other team. In the NBA the 3-point line is 23 feet 9 inches from the middle of the hoop to a spot just above the top of the key. The arc is the same distance except for the straight line part, which is 3 feet from the sidelines. Then it measures 22 feet from the middle of the hoop out to the 3-point line.

A 3-pointer is a riskier shot because of the distance, but does that risk pay off? A 3-pointer gets 1.5 times the value of a 2-point shot (3 / 2 = 1.5). You could also say that a 3-pointer is worth 50 percent more points than a 2-pointer.

While the NBA measures 23 feet 9 inches for the 3-point line, college 3-point lines are only 20 feet 9 inches, and most high schools measure 19 feet 9 inches.

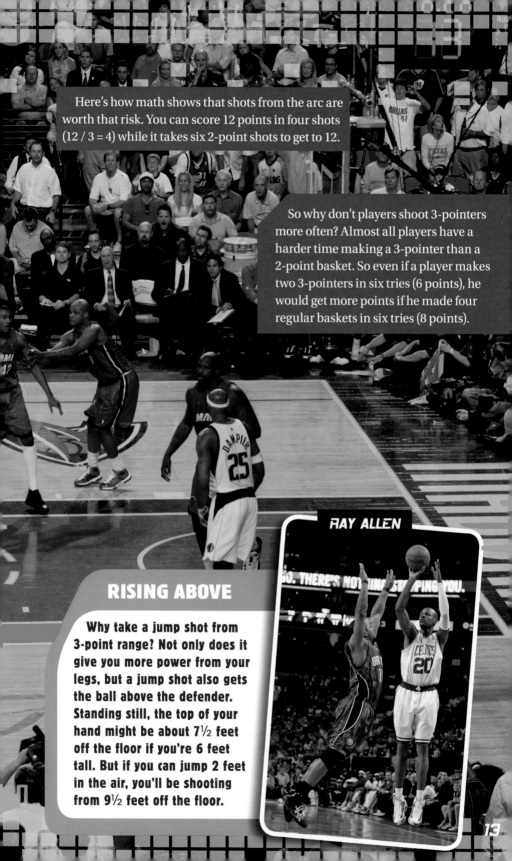

Here's how math shows that shots from the arc are worth that risk. You can score 12 points in four shots (12 / 3 = 4) while it takes six 2-point shots to get to 12.

So why don't players shoot 3-pointers more often? Almost all players have a harder time making a 3-pointer than a 2-point basket. So even if a player makes two 3-pointers in six tries (6 points), he would get more points if he made four regular baskets in six tries (8 points).

RAY ALLEN

RISING ABOVE

Why take a jump shot from 3-point range? Not only does it give you more power from your legs, but a jump shot also gets the ball above the defender. Standing still, the top of your hand might be about $7\frac{1}{2}$ feet off the floor if you're 6 feet tall. But if you can jump 2 feet in the air, you'll be shooting from $9\frac{1}{2}$ feet off the floor.

CHAPTER 2

POINTS PER GAME

In sports a lot of stats show averages. In basketball the most common average statistic is a player's points per game. The scoring leader of the 2010–2011 season was Kevin Durant of the Oklahoma City Thunder. He scored 2,161 over the course of the season. It's easier to tell how much he contributed if we look at the average points he scored each night. To do that, divide his total points by the number of games he played.

KEVIN DURANT

$$\frac{2{,}161 \text{ points}}{78 \text{ games}} = 27.7 \text{ PPG}$$

When talking about scoring averages in basketball, you have to include the numbers Michael Jordan put up during his career. Air Jordan scored 32,292 points and played in 1,072 games. With just that information, we can calculate his career average points per game.

$$\text{PPG} = \frac{32{,}292}{1{,}072}$$

Jordan's career PPG = 30.1

MICHAEL JORDAN

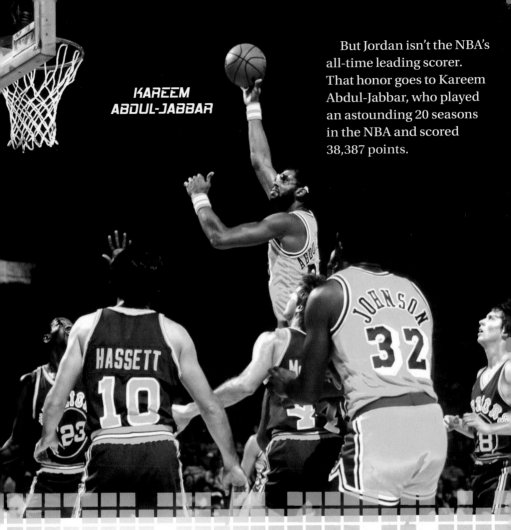

KAREEM ABDUL-JABBAR

But Jordan isn't the NBA's all-time leading scorer. That honor goes to Kareem Abdul-Jabbar, who played an astounding 20 seasons in the NBA and scored 38,387 points.

Abdul-Jabbar played in 1,560 games. His average PPG over his career was 24.6 (38,387 / 1,560). Let's compare the career stats of Jordan and Abdul-Jabbar in a chart.

Abdul-Jabbar scored more points overall than Jordan, but Jordan's averages are higher because he played in fewer games and fewer seasons. Even though Jordan isn't the NBA's all-time leading scorer for overall points scored, he does lead the NBA in career points per game.

	MICHAEL JORDAN	KAREEM ABDUL-JABBAR
POINTS	32,292	38,387
GAMES	1,072	1,560
SEASONS	15	20
PPG	30.1	24.6
POINTS/ SEASON	2,152.8	1,919.4

SCORING DISTRIBUTION

A basketball team relies on more than just one player. For a team to succeed, it needs good contributions from all its players, including those who come off the bench. No stat is perfect at showing the value of a team's subs, but scoring distribution can give us some idea. We can find out what percentage of a team's points each player scored. If a high percentage of points was scored by the starting five, then that team might not have a very deep bench.

On January 3, 2011, eight Orlando Magic players scored in double digits for all 110 of the Magic's points.

PLAYER	POINTS	% OF TOTAL TEAM PTS
H. TURKOGLU	10	9%
B. BASS	10	9%
D. HOWARD	22	20%
J. RICHARDSON	20	18%
J. NELSON	11	10%
J. REDICK	13	12%
R. ANDERSON	13	12%
G. ARENAS	11	10%
TOTAL	110	100%

HEDO TURKOGLU

DWYANE WADE

In another game from the same day, the Miami Heat had nine players score points, but the distribution was quite different.

Three players scored 84 percent of the Heat's points. But in the Magic game, no player scored more than 20 percent of the team's points.

PLAYER	POINTS	% OF TOTAL TEAM PTS
L. JAMES	38	40%
C. BOSH	11	11%
Z. ILGAUSKAS	2	2%
D. WADE	31	33%
C. ARROYO	2	2%
J. JONES	6	6%
J. ANTHONY	2	2%
J. HOWARD	2	2%
M. CHALMERS	2	2%
TOTAL	96	100%

HIGH SCORERS

The most points scored in an NBA game was 370. On December 13, 1983, the Pistons beat the Nuggets 186-184 in triple overtime. With 5 minutes for each overtime added to the 48 minutes of regulation play, that's 63 minutes of playing time. The two teams together scored 5.87 points per minute! (370 / 63 = 5.87)

PERCENTAGES

How many points players score only tells part of the story. One way to see how efficient they are at scoring is to look at their field goal percentage.

Let's take a look at Kevin Love's stats for a single game. On January 17, 2011, Love scored 31 points for the Minnesota Timberwolves against the Oklahoma City Thunder. In that game he took 23 shots and made 13. What was his FG%?

To calculate FG% you need to know how many field goals were attempted (FGA) and how many were made (FGM).

FG% = FGM / FGA

FG% = 13 / 23

FG% = .5652

KEVIN LOVE

To turn this number into a percentage, multiply by 100. An easy way to multiply a number by 100 is to move the decimal point two places to the right. All that's left is to add the % symbol.

FG% = 56.52%

Love had a great average—anything over 50 percent is considered good. But during a game earlier that month, he took 12 shots and made only five. He scored 11 points. That's a FG% of only 41.66 percent (5 / 12 = .4416). This just shows that a player's FG% and other stats can change over the course of the season. So for a true test of how well a player is doing in a season, you need more data, not just information from one or two games.

By the end of the season, Kevin Love shot 1,026 FG and made 482 of them. What was his FG% at the end of the season?

ANSWER: 47%

Interested in free throws? To calculate a player's free throw percentage, take the number of free throws made and divide it by the number of free throws attempted.

Steve Nash of the Phoenix Suns attempted 249 free throws during the 2010–2011 season and made 227 of them. What was his field goal percentage?

ANSWER: 91.2%

STEVE NASH

We can do more with percentages by analyzing stats from one game. Here are key numbers from a game on March 9, 2011, between the New York Knicks and the Memphis Grizzlies.

KNICKS			
POINTS FROM 2-PT FGs	POINTS FROM 3s	POINTS FROM FTs	TOTAL POINTS
70	36	4	110

GRIZZLIES			
POINTS FROM 2-PT FGs	POINTS FROM 3s	POINTS FROM FTs	TOTAL POINTS
66	9	33	108

Let's turn this data into pie charts to help us take a closer look:

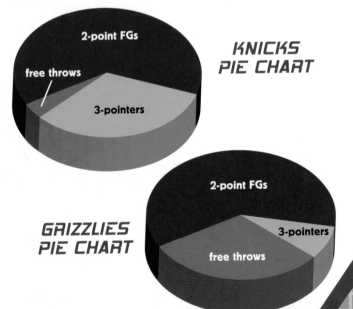

2-point FGs
free throws
3-pointers

KNICKS PIE CHART

2-point FGs
3-pointers
free throws

GRIZZLIES PIE CHART

What percentage of the points came from 2-point FGs?

KNICKS:
70 / 110 = .636, or 63.6%

GRIZZLIES:
66 / 108 = .611, or 61.1%

Both teams have a similar percentage for points from 2-point field goals, but what percentage of the points were scored from the free throw line?

KNICKS:

4 / 110 = .036, or 3.6%

GRIZZLIES:

33 / 108 = .305, or 30.5%

MIKE CONLEY

Now let's look at the points from 3-pointers.

KNICKS:

36 / 110 = .327, or 32.7%

GRIZZLIES:

9 / 108 = .083, or 8.3%

CARMELO ANTHONY

So how did the Knicks come out with the win? Even though the Grizzlies outscored the Knicks by 29 points from the free throw line, the difference came from the 3-point line. The Knicks made nine more 3-pointers than the Grizzlies, which is a 27-point swing. The four-point advantage in 2-point field goals for the Knicks was enough for the win.

EFFECTIVE FG%

Now that you know how to calculate a player's FG%, let's go one step further: the effective FG%. Suppose during one quarter of a game, the center shoots three for five for a total of 6 points scored. In the same quarter, the point guard sinks two of five 3-pointers. The center's FG% is 60%, but the point guard's is only 40%. However, they each scored 6 points in five shots taken. The problem is that the normal FG% stat doesn't give any credit for 3-pointers.

The effective FG% stat uses a formula to make each 3-pointer worth 1½ made shots. Where did that number come from? The ratio between a 3-pointer and a 2-pointer is 3:2. Expressed as a fraction, that's 3/2, or 1.5.

WHO NEEDS THREES?

Dwight Howard of the Orlando Magic was one of the league leaders in effective field goal percentage in the 2010–2011 season. But he didn't make any 3-pointers. His FG% alone was awesome enough to have one of the best effective FG%. Both stats were .593.

DWIGHT HOWARD

In a San Antonio Spurs game during the 2010–2011 season, Manu Ginobili hit four of 10 3-pointers and eight of 17 field goals overall. His teammate Tony Parker hit seven of 16 field goals, nailing one of three from the 3-point arc. To find their effective FG%, plug their stats into this formula.

$$(FG + .5 * 3\text{-}pointers) / FGA$$

Remember the order of operations when you solve the equation. Start with what's in the parentheses. Multiplication comes before addition in the order of operations, so we'll calculate that first.

$$(8 + (.5 * 4) / 17$$
$$(8 + 2) / 17$$
$$10 / 17 = .588$$

MANU GINOBILI

$$(7 + (.5 * 1) / 16$$
$$(7 + .5) / 16$$
$$7.5 / 16 = .469$$

TONY PARKER

These two players had similar FG%, but their effective FG% were very different. Once Ginobili gets credit for his 3-pointers, his effectiveness goes up. This stat rewards those who risk low-percentage shots because the return is higher if they can make even 40 percent of the shots.

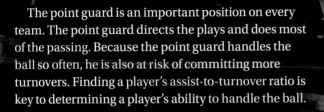

ASSIST/TURNOVER RATIO

The point guard is an important position on every team. The point guard directs the plays and does most of the passing. Because the point guard handles the ball so often, he is also at risk of committing more turnovers. Finding a player's assist-to-turnover ratio is key to determining a player's ability to handle the ball.

CHRIS PAUL

Chris Paul is an elite point guard. In the 2010–2011 season with the New Orleans Hornets, he had 782 assists and 177 turnovers. Here's how to calculate his assist-to-turnover ratio.

$$AST / TO = 782 / 177 = 4.42$$

For every TO Paul committed, he had 4.42 assists to make up for it. Even though he came in fourth for assists per game, he had the league's best assist-to-turnover ratio.

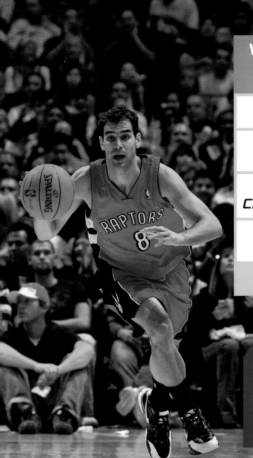

Which of these three players had the best assist-to-turnover ratio during the 2010–2011 season!

	ASSISTS	TURNOVERS
STEVE NASH	855	265
JOSE CALDERON	605	148
JASON KIDD	655	179

ANSWER: Jose Calderon
(Calderon, 4.09; Kidd, 3.66; Nash, 3.23)

Can the AST/TO ratio ever be negative? No. But if a player commits more turnovers than assists, then the ratio goes below 1. For example, if a player has 60 assists and 95 turnovers, his AST/TO ratio is 0.63. That player likely isn't ready to be a point guard.

MAKING IT COUNT

TV announcers often talk about another interesting stat called points off turnovers. It shows how many points a team scores after turnovers. It's not just a matter of forcing a turnover—you've got to score some points!

LEBRON JAMES

CHAPTER 3

MEAN, MEDIAN, MODE, AND RANGE

There are a lot of ways to look at numbers to see how a player is doing over a certain time period. It's useful to see how a player did over a particular month. Here are the scoring numbers for Amar'e Stoudemire of the New York Knicks for January 2011.

Let's start with his scoring average for the month. The mathematical word for average is mean. Figure out Stoudemire's mean scoring for January 2011.

DATE	POINTS SCORED
JAN 2	26
JAN 4	28
JAN 7	23
JAN 9	23
JAN 11	23
JAN 12	22
JAN 14	25
JAN 17	41
JAN 19	25
JAN 21	18
JAN 22	18
JAN 24	30
JAN 27	24
JAN 28	27
JAN 30	33

$$mean = \frac{total\ points}{games\ played}$$

$$mean = \frac{386\ points}{15\ games}$$

$$mean = 25.7\ PPG$$

Other stats we can find out in a list of numbers like this are the median, mode, and range.

mean—the average amount of a set of numbers

median—the middle number in a list of numbers

mode—the number in a list that is repeated most often

range—the difference between the largest and smallest value

The best way to find these stats is to organize Stoudemire's scores from lowest to highest.

18, 18, 22, 23, 23, 23, 24, 25, 25, 26, 27, 28, 30, 33, 41

The number in the middle of the list is 25. Although 25 is not exactly halfway between the lowest and highest scores (18 and 41), it's very close to the average PPG (25.7).

Now let's look at the mode. There is one score that shows up three times: 23. Since no other score shows up four or more times, 23 is the mode.

To figure out Stoudemire's range that month, subtract the lowest number from the highest number.

$$41 - 18 = 23$$

What does that mean for Stoudemire's scoring that month? It means he was consistent. He usually scored in the mid-20s.

AMAR'E STOUDEMIRE

Do mean, median, mode, and range always work out to be this close? Suppose a player over the same 15 games had the scoring output below.

6, 8, 8, 8, 8, 8, 15, 17, 27, 42, 43, 44, 47, 56, 66

These stats are unrealistic, but here's how the analysis breaks down.

mean = 403 / 15 = 26.9

median: 17

mode: 8

range: 60

These numbers show that the player is extremely inconsistent.

CALCULATING CHANGE

We can use math to put a number on how much players improve. For example, Joakim Noah of the Chicago Bulls pulled down an average of 7.6 rebounds per game during the 2008–2009 season. For the 2009–2010 season, he increased his rebounding average to 11 rebounds per game, an increase of 3.4 RB per game. This looks even more impressive when we calculate it as a percentage.

To find the percent increase, first find the difference between the two numbers.

$$11.0 - 7.6 = 3.4$$

Then take the result and divide it by the original number.

$$3.4 / 7.6 = .4474, \text{ or } 44.74\%$$

That improvement is truly impressive!

JOAKIM NOAH

You do the math the same way to find percent decrease. For example, when Kevin Garnett was with the Timberwolves, he was the team's leading scorer. During the 2006–2007 season, he averaged 22.4 points per game. The next season he was traded to the Boston Celtics. There he played beside two other high-scoring players: Paul Pierce and Ray Allen. Garnett's PPG during the 2007–2008 season dropped to 18.8. What was his percent decrease?

$$18.8 - 22.4 = -3.6$$

$$-3.6 / 22.4 = -.1607, \text{ or } -16\%$$

Although Garnett's PPG went down, his FG% went up. Because opposing players had to worry about Pierce and Allen as well, Garnett was able to take better shots.

COMPARING STATS

You can use numbers more than one way to make comparisons between players. Let's compare the rebounds for two stars during the 2010–2011 season.

	BLAKE GRIFFIN	ZACH RANDOLPH
OFFENSIVE REBOUNDS	270	326
DEFENSIVE REBOUNDS	719	588
TOTAL REBOUNDS	989	914

Blake Griffin had more total rebounds than Zach Randolph, but Randolph had more offensive rebounds. Let's make that a percent so we can compare the stats easier.

First we need to express the numbers as fractions. Offensive rebounds go in the numerator, and total rebounds go in the denominator.

GRIFFIN:
$$\frac{270}{989}$$

RANDOLPH:
$$\frac{326}{914}$$

Then turn the fractions into decimals through division.

GRIFFIN:
$$\frac{270}{989} = 27.3\%$$

RANDOLPH:
$$\frac{326}{914} = 35.7\%$$

While 27.3 percent of Griffin's rebounds were on offense, Randolph had 35.7 percent in the same category. From these stats, it's easy to see that Randolph was better than Griffin at muscling for offensive boards that season.

BLAKE GRIFFIN

You can also compare fractions without finding the percentages. First you have to find the lowest common denominator between the fractions. The lowest common denominator is the lowest number that the denominators of both fractions can be divided into evenly.

In a 2010–2011 game, the Sacramento Kings' DeMarcus Cousins went six for 18 from the field. In the same game, Devin Harris of the Utah Jazz went five for 12. Because Cousins took more shots, it's hard to tell which player had a better shooting night. That's where the common denominator comes in. The lowest common denominator for those two numbers is 36.

To calculate the numerators, you have to figure out how many times the denominators go into the lowest common denominator. In this case, 18 goes into 36 two times, and 12 goes into 36 three times. So you multiple Cousins' numerator by two and Harris' numerator by three.

COUSINS:

$$\frac{6 * 2}{18 * 2} = \frac{12}{36}$$

HARRIS:

$$\frac{5 * 3}{12 * 3} = \frac{15}{36}$$

The fractions represent how many baskets the two players would have made out of 36 shots (based on how many shots they made during the game). Because the denominators are equal, it's easy to compare the fractions. Harris had a better shooting night.

DEMARCUS COUSINS

PROJECTIONS

We can use math to make predictions. You can guess what is likely to happen to players throughout the course of a game or season. For example, let's say Monta Ellis of the Golden State Warriors scores six points in the first quarter. How many points is he on pace to score in the game? Cross multiplication can show us the answer.

Knowing that there are four quarters in a game and a player scored six points in the first quarter and 10 points in the second quarter, we can state the problem like this: 16 points is to two quarters as x points is to four quarters. Using cross multiplication, it looks like this:

$$\frac{16}{2} = \frac{x}{4}$$

Now we solve for x, the number of points expected after four quarters. Start by multiplying the numerator of one fraction by the denominator of the other.

Then divide each side by 2 to get x by itself.

$$16 * 4 = 2 * x$$
$$64 = 2x$$

$$64 / 2 = x$$
$$x = 32$$

In a single game, a player's scoring can vary. Ellis could score only two points in the third quarter. If he catches fire in the fourth quarter with 18 points, he would end the game with 36 points. Although his scoring wasn't consistent in each quarter, using cross multiplication gives us an estimate of what his final points scored will be for the game.

You can use cross multiplication to project what a player's end-of-the-season stats are as well. Derrick Rose of the Chicago Bulls began the 2010–2011 season with these scoring numbers over the first 10 games: 28, 39, 16, 24, 18, 18, 22, 24, 33, 33 = 255.

From those 10 games, how many points is he on pace to score for the season? (There are 82 games in a season.)

$$\frac{255}{10} = \frac{x}{82}$$

$$255 * 82 = 10 * x$$
$$20{,}910 = 10x$$

$$20{,}910 / 10 = x$$
$$x = 2{,}091$$

Using cross multiplication, we can predict that Rose would score 2,091 points over the whole season. And that's only using the stats from his first 10 games. In fact, Rose scored 2,026 points, so the estimate was very close!

POINTS PER 100 POSSESSIONS

Statisticians have worked on ways to measure how well teams are performing throughout the season. These measurements help predict who might win games, make the playoffs, or if an upset is possible. One of these stats is called a team's points per 100 possessions.

Calculating this stat is tricky. First we need to define what a possession is. It's when a team has control of the ball, right? But what if a team grabs a defensive rebound and then commits a turnover right away? Does that count as a possession? Statisticians came up with a formula to determine a team's number of possessions during a game. It includes the team's field goal attempts, turnovers, offensive rebounds, and free throw attempts.

$$possessions = FGA + TO - ORB + (FTA * .44)$$

Where does the FTA * .44 part come from? Free throws attempted need to be figured in, but not every single one. Not all free throws end a team's possession of the ball. In fact, by analyzing stats over time, mathematicians figured out that about 44 percent of free throws end the team's possession.

Let's try the formula using the Lakers' 2009–2010 championship team as an example. First we need to know a few basic stats.

FGA	6,875
TO	1,096
ORB	973
FTA	1,985

Then plug the numbers into the formula.

$$possessions = 6,875 + 1,096 - 973 + (1,985 * .44)$$
$$possessions = 6,875 + 1,096 - 973 + 873.4$$
$$possessions = 7,871.4$$

Once you figure out number of possessions, you can calculate points per possession. The Lakers scored a total of 8,339 points that season.

$$points\ per\ possession = \frac{8,339}{7,871.4} = 1.06$$

Multiply the result by 100 to get points per 100 possessions. One hundred is a good estimate for how many possessions a team gets each game. The final stat then ends up looking like a game score by which we can compare the team to other teams.

The Lakers had 106 points per 100 possessions that season. That was 11th in the league! So this stat alone might not tell you who will win the Finals. Try some match-ups throughout the season and see how teams compare.

CHAPTER 4

GAME STATS

People keep track of a lot of different stats for every NBA game. Those stats need to be shown in an easy-to-read manner so fans can quickly pick out information from each game. Bar graphs and tables help organize this information. Let's look at a game played between the Celtics and Knicks on December 15, 2010.

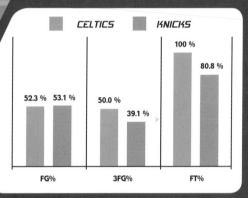

CELTICS VS. KNICKS GAME STATS

You can see at a glance a lot of information about this game. Which team had the better FG%? Which team had the better FT%?

These stats are fun to look at and compare, but in the pros, teams need wins. Can you tell from this information who won the game? You might guess that since the Celtics led in almost every category that they won the game. In this case, you would be correct. But the stats don't tell you that the game came down to the last second. Paul Pierce of the Celtics hit a jumper with 0.4 seconds left to take the lead. Amar'e Stoudemire of the Knicks then hit a 3-pointer at the buzzer, but it was too late and didn't count. The Celtics won 118-116.

Now look at this summary from December 18, 2010, between the Memphis Grizzlies and San Antonio Spurs.

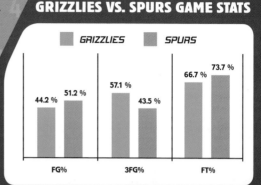

GRIZZLIES VS. SPURS GAME STATS

GRIZZLIES SPURS

FG%: 44.2 % / 51.2 %
3FG%: 57.1 % / 43.5 %
FT%: 66.7 % / 73.7 %

GRIZZLIES VS. SPURS

Looking at the game stats, would you be able to guess who won? The Memphis Grizzlies had a better 3-point FG%. But the San Antonio Spurs had a better FG% and FT%. Each team excelled at different aspects of the game. In fact, it was a close game—the Spurs won in overtime. The one stat that really matters is the final score!

A team's ability to win on the road is key to success. With half of their games away from home, a team needs to do well on the road to have a winning season.

In 2009–2010 the Charlotte Bobcats had a great home record of 31–10. But their road record was a dismal 13–28. While their home record was one of the best in their division, their road record prevented them from getting better than a seventh seed for the playoffs.

CHARLOTTE
BOBCATS

Let's use math to find a way to quickly gauge teams' home and road performances and compare teams in one division from that season. Here are the records for the Southeast Division for the 2009–2010 season.

SOUTHEAST	W–L	HOME	ROAD
ORLANDO	59–23	34–7	25–16
ATLANTA	53–29	34–7	19–22
MIAMI	47–35	24–17	23–18
CHARLOTTE	44–38	31–10	13–28
WASHINGTON	26–56	15–26	11–30

We can think of these W–L records in terms of positive and negative numbers. Look at Atlanta's home record. Subtract the losses from the wins: (34 – 7 = 27). Their home record is +27 because they won 27 more games than they lost at home. On the other hand, their road record (19 – 22 = -3) was much worse. On the road they lost more games than they won. Charlotte had almost as good a home record as division leaders Orlando and Atlanta: +21 vs. +27. But for a road record, only one team was worse: Charlotte's -15 vs. Washington's -19.

ATLANTA HAWKS

There's another good use of positive and negative numbers in basketball. We can use a team's average points per game minus opponents' average points per game to get the difference. With this stat you get a general idea about a team's offensive power and defensive ability.

ORLANDO MAGIC

For example, in 2009–2010 the Orlando Magic scored an average of 102.8 points per game. Their opponents scored an average of 95.3 points per game against them. Subtract the two to get the difference.

$$102.8 = 95.3 = +7.5$$

That was the NBA's best that season. On the other hand, the Minnesota Timberwolves scored an average of 98.2 points per game, and their opponents scored an average of 107.8 points per game against them.

$$98.2 = 107.8 = -9.6$$

That was the worst in the NBA that season.

MINNESOTA TIMBERWOLVES

THE POSTSEASON

In the NBA 16 teams go to the playoffs. There are 30 teams in the league, so what percentage of all teams go to the playoffs? This is just like calculating FG%. Divide the number of teams that go to the playoffs by the total number of teams.

$$16 / 30 = .533$$

That's 53.3 percent. Just over half of the teams make it to the postseason. However, it's a long road from the first round of the playoffs to the NBA Finals. Each round is a best of seven series. That means two teams will play up to seven games to find out which team advances. The first team to win four games advances to the next round of the playoffs. To win the championship, a team has to do that four times. Multiply the two numbers (4 * 4), and you get the number of wins needed to take home the championship (16).

In the 2009–2010 season, the LA Lakers defeated the Celtics in the Finals in Game 7. But it took more than 16 games to get there. They played a total of 23 playoff games.

Metta World Peace

Let's put that into perspective. They also played 82 regular season games. What percentage of their games played were playoff games?

$$\frac{playoff\ games}{total\ games} = \begin{array}{c} percentage \\ of\ total \end{array}$$

$$23 / (23 + 82)$$
$$23 / 105 = 22\%$$

More than one-fifth of their games were playoff games! After a long 82-game season, did the Lakers step it up in the playoffs? The Lakers were 57–25 during the regular season. Win percentage is a quick calculation.

$$win\ percentage = \frac{wins}{(wins + losses)}$$

$$57 / (57 + 25)$$
$$57 / 82 = .695$$

Now let's look at their playoff games to see how their win percentage changed. Their playoff record ended up at 16–7 (three of those losses to the Celtics in the Finals).

$$16 / (16 + 7)$$
$$16 / 23 = .696$$

The playoff win percentage is almost the same as the regular season win percentage. The Lakers simply played solid ball all season.

MARCH MADNESS

The pros don't get all the basketball attention. Millions of fans from across the country watch the men's and women's college national championship tournaments. But March Madness also brings about interesting numbers.

With the best college teams playing for a championship, there are plenty of buzzer beaters, upsets, and dramatic plays to watch. For three straight weeks, you can watch your fill of college ball. But how many total games are played during the tournament?

The men's tournament starts out with 68 teams. The first round (the First Four) features eight teams going head-to-head. The winners advance to the second round, where 64 teams play 32 games. After the second round, there will be half as many teams (32). That means there are 16 games in the third round, eight games in the fourth round, and four games in the fifth round. The sixth round features the last four teams (the Final Four) in two games. The last two teams square off in the championship game.

The total games is one less than the number of teams that started the tournament. That makes sense because only one team remains undefeated in the tournament.

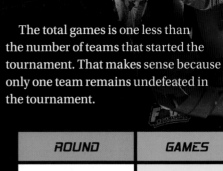

ROUND	GAMES
FIRST FOUR	4
SECOND ROUND	32
THIRD ROUND	16
SWEET 16	8
ELITE EIGHT	4
FINAL FOUR	2
CHAMPIONSHIP	1
TOTAL GAMES	67

How many consecutive games must the champ win? How about if the team also has to play in the First Four round?

ANSWER: six, seven

The women's tournament doesn't have a First Four round. With only 64 teams in the tournament, 63 games are played.

Don't let the numbers fool you. Although a No. 1 seeded team has never lost its first game, only once have all four No. 1 seeds made it to the Final Four (2008). In 2011 the NCAA men's tournament was without a No. 1 or 2 seed in the Final Four. It was the first time in March Madness history.

SALARIES

Pro athletes make a lot of money, and NBA players are no exception. It could be argued that Dirk Nowitzki's salary for 2009–2010 of about $18 million is worth it. He has helped the Dallas Mavericks to 10 straight playoff appearances. But for most of us, that's a mind-boggling amount of money to play a game!

During that season, Nowitzki played in 81 games. How much money did he make per game?

$$\$18,000,000 / 81 = \$222,222$$

This gets more incredible when you figure that Nowitzki played a total of 3,039 minutes that season. That's $5,923 per minute on the court!

Let's find out how much Nowitzki was paid per point he scored for his team. He scored 2,027 points during the regular season.

$$\$18,000,000 / 2,027 = \$8,880$$

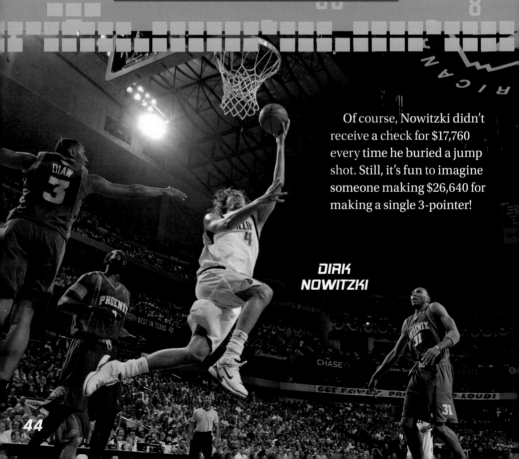

Of course, Nowitzki didn't receive a check for $17,760 every time he buried a jump shot. Still, it's fun to imagine someone making $26,640 for making a single 3-pointer!

DIRK NOWITZKI

Let's see how Nowitzki's pay compares to the season's scoring leader, Kevin Durant of the Oklahoma City Thunder. Durant led the NBA in scoring with 30.1 points per game. Here's how the two players compared.

2009–2010 SEASON STATS	DIRK NOWITZKI	KEVIN DURANT
SALARY (APPROXIMATE)	$18,000,000	$4,800,000
TOTAL POINTS	2,027	2,472
GAMES PLAYED	81	82
MINUTES PLAYED	3,039	3,239
SALARY PER GAME	$222,222	$58,537
SALARY PER MINUTE	$5,923	$1,482
SALARY PER POINT	$8,880	$1,942

Because Nowitzki's salary is almost four times greater than Durant's, the salary per game, minute, and point is very different between the two players. So why is Nowitzki's salary so much higher? There are a lot of reasons, but one reason is consistency. During that season, Durant had only been in the league for three years, and Nowitzki had been a pro for 12 years. Players are often paid more if they play well consistently over many seasons.

KEVIN DURANT

THE NBA PLAYOFFS POOL

The NBA rewards teams that make the playoffs. Bonuses are paid out from a pool. For the 2009–2010 season, the pool was worth $12 million. Each team that makes the first round of the playoffs gets a bonus of $179,092. The team that wins the championship gets $2,125,137. That bonus is split among the players and coaches.

GLOSSARY

area—the amount of surface within a specific boundary; area is measured in square units

denominator—the bottom number in a fraction

diameter—the length of a straight line through the center of a circle

dimension—an object's measurement or size; an object's dimensions are length, width, and height

mean—the average amount of a set of numbers

median—the middle number in a list of numbers

mode—the number in a list that is repeated the most often

numerator—the top number in a fraction

order of operations—a rule used to solve the parts of a mathematical equation in the correct order; the order of operations is parentheses, exponents, multiplication and division, and addition and subtraction

perimeter—the outside edge around a specific area

radius—the length of a line drawn from the middle of a circle to the edge

range—the difference between the largest and smallest value in a list of numbers

ratio—a comparison of two quantities expressed in numbers

right angle—a 90-degree angle

READ MORE

Mahaney, Ian F. *The Math of Basketball.* Sports Math. New York: PowerKids Press, 2011.

Minden, Cecilia, and Katie Marsico. *Basketball.* Real World Math, Sports. Ann Arbor, Mich.: Cherry Lake Pub., 2009.

Woods, Mark, and Ruth Owen. *Slam Dunk!: Basketball Facts and Stats.* Top Score Math. New York: Gareth Stevens Pub., 2011.

INTERNET SITES

FactHound offers a safe, fun way to find Internet sites related to this book. All of the sites on FactHound have been researched by our staff.

Here's all you do:

Visit *www.facthound.com*

Type in this code: 9781429665681

Super-cool stuff!

Check out projects, games and lots more at
www.capstonekids.com

INDEX